LIFE SKILLS

GIRLS' GUIDE TO FEELING FABULOUS!

Barbara Sheen

Heinemann
LIBRARY

www.heinemannlibrary.co.uk
Visit our website to find out more
information about Heinemann
Library books.

To order:
☎ Phone +44 (0) 1865 888066
🖺 Fax +44 (0) 1865 314091
💻 Visit www.heinemannlibrary.co.uk

Heinemann Library is an imprint of Capstone Global
Library Limited, a company incorporated in England
and Wales having its registered office at 7 Pilgrim
Street, London, EC4V 6LB – Registered company
number: 6695582

Heinemann is a registered trademark of Pearson
Education Limited, under licence to Capstone Global
Library Limited

Edited by Pollyanna Poulter
Designed by Philippa Jenkins and Hart MacLeod
Picture research by Elizabeth Alexander and
    Maria Joannou
Production by Alison Parsons
Originated by Modern Age Repro House Ltd.
Printed and bound in China by South China
    Printing Company Ltd.

ISBN 978 0 431112 44 2 (hardback)
13 12 11 10 09
10 9 8 7 6 5 4 3 2 1

ISBN 978 0 431112 60 2 (paperback)
15 14 13 12 11
10 9 8 7 6 5 4 3 2 1

British Library Cataloguing-in-Publication Data
Sheen, Barbara
Girls' guide to feeling fabulous! - (Life skills)
613'.04242
A full catalogue record for this book is available
from the British Library.

Acknowledgements
We would like to thank the following for
permission to reproduce photographs: © Alamy:
pp. 5 (Buzzshotz), 9 (Avatra Images), 14
(Jupiterimages/Polka Dot), 33 (UpperCut Images),
37 (RubberBall); © Corbis: pp. 12 (Dex Images),
16 (Tom Stewart), 41 (Rob Melnychuk/Brand X);
© Getty Images: pp. 20 (Image Bank/John Kelly),
22 (Allsports/Nathan Bilow), 25 (Stock4B/Sabine
Fritsch), 34 (Image Bank/Paolo Curto), 42 (Taxi/
Yellow Dog Productions), 45 (Look/Frank van
Groen); © Masterfile: pp. 27 (Horst Herget), 49
(David Schmidt); © Photolibrary: pp. 7 (Foodpix),
18 (BSIP Medical), 29 (Flirt Collection); © Rex
Features: pp. 31 (Action Press), 39 (Sipa Press),
47 (Francis Dean).

Cover photograph of young Asian woman holding
bunch of green leaf vegetables reproduced with
permission of © Punchstock (Blend Images).

We would like to thank Anne E. Pezalla for her
invaluable help in the preparation of this book.

Every effort has been made to contact copyright
holders of material reproduced in this book. Any
omissions will be rectified in subsequent printings
if notice is given to the Publishers.

Contents

Some words are printed in bold, **like this**. You can find out
what they mean by looking in the glossary.

Take Care Of Yourself

Feeling great is about taking care of yourself on the inside as well as on the outside. As you become a young woman, you grow and change both physically and emotionally.

CHALLENGING TIMES

Although this is an exciting time, it is also challenging and confusing. It is hard to know what is normal when you are uncertain whether other girls are experiencing the same physical changes and mixture of emotions. Because of all that you are going through, it is not unusual to feel happy, sad, angry, anxious, **self-conscious**, then happy again all within a few hours.

With so much going on, it is difficult to know where you fit in and what your place is in the world. You will be faced with many decisions, and sometimes you may feel as if your life is out of control. Some days it may be hard to know who you are at the moment, not to mention what kind of person you will become.

Taking control

Although you cannot change the fact that you are growing up, you can take steps to make the process easier and put yourself in control. The way you respond to the changes in your body, the way you act around other people, and the choices you make all influence the person you are now and the woman you will become. Taking care of and respecting yourself both physically and emotionally gives you this control and helps you to feel great!

• CHECKLIST •

Don't feel strange if you wonder about the following questions – all girls ask them, and this book will help answer them.

- When will I get my period? How much bleeding is normal? Why is my period irregular?

- Why are my breasts uneven? Will they even out? Will they ever grow?

- Why do my parents treat me like a baby? Why don't they trust me or listen to me?

- Why don't I have more friends? Why is my best friend ignoring me?

What you do defines who you are more than what you say. For example, you say you care about your friend. But if you choose to watch your favourite television programme, rather than help him or her with their maths homework when they ask you to, your actions do not show that you care. If you promise to get more exercise, then ask your mum to drive you to school, your actions again do not match your words. Compare what you say with what you do. Your words and your actions should be the same.

You are becoming a young woman. The changes you are going through can be difficult to deal with, but you can feel in control by understanding those changes. They are exciting and normal!

You Are What You Eat

What and how much you eat affects the way you look and feel. Eating properly is one of the best things you can do for your body.

EATING A BALANCED DIET

One of the simplest steps you can take to feel terrific is to eat a balanced diet. Eating a variety of foods ensures you get all the **nutrients** you need. These include proteins, carbohydrates, fats, vitamins, and minerals. (See the chart below for more information on where nutrients are found and the benefits they bring.)

A typical balanced meal might consist of: meat or fish (for protein and fat), pasta, rice, or bread (for carbohydrates), vegetables and fresh fruit (for vitamins and minerals), and a glass of milk.

A good way to judge whether you are getting a variety of nutrients is to look at the colours on your plate. The more colours, the more nutrients you are probably getting (this does not apply to brightly coloured sweets!). That is why low-fat yoghurt mixed with blueberries, strawberries, banana, nuts, and granola makes an excellent light meal or snack. It is delicious, nutritious, and colourful.

The nutrients you need		
Nutrient	Found in	What does it do?
Protein	Meat, fish, seafood, poultry, milk, eggs, nuts, beans.	Repairs and builds muscles and cells.
Carbohydrate	Bread, cereal, pasta, rice, nuts, beans, sugar.	Provides energy.
Fat	Dairy products, oils, nuts, meat, fish, poultry.	Provides energy and keeps the body warm.
Vitamin	Fruits, vegetables, grains, nuts, meat, dairy products.	Fights disease, keeps skin, eyes, and hair healthy.
Mineral	Fruits, vegetables, nuts, dairy products, grains, beans, meat, fish.	Fights disease, builds bones and teeth, helps blood production.

YOU CAN DO IT!

Make a nutrient-rich smoothie

A smoothie is delicious and good for you, too. To make this recipe you will need:

- *a blender*
- *200g fresh or frozen fruit (such as strawberries, peaches, or bananas), sliced*
- *100ml plain or vanilla low-fat yoghurt*
- *100ml low-fat milk*
- *1 teaspoon honey (optional)*

1. Blend all the ingredients until a smooth liquid forms.
2. Pour the liquid into a glass.
3. Add some ice cubes. What a delicious snack!

Adding fibre

Fibre keeps you healthy by moving food through your **digestive system**. You can get more fibre in your diet by eating **whole grains**, nuts, beans, seeds, vegetables, and fruits. Try sprinkling almonds and raisins on cereal, tossing a sliced tomato with pasta, or topping a sandwich with bean sprouts.

Healthy cooking

How you cook your food also affects its nutritional value. If you boil, roast, or grill food – rather than frying it in butter or oil – no excess fat is added. Steaming vegetables gives them a crunchy taste and keeps in the vitamins that boiling can remove.

If a meal is made from naturally colourful ingredients, it probably has a good variety of nutrients.

Choose carbohydrates wisely

When you decide what to eat, keep in mind that there are two kinds of carbohydrate: complex and simple. Which type you choose affects how you feel. Complex carbohydrates give you long-lasting **energy** that keeps you feeling strong for hours. You get complex carbohydrates in grains, potatoes, nuts, and beans.

Simple carbohydrates give you a short burst of energy that does not last. Sugary foods like sweets and cake are full of simple carbohydrates. The sugar in these foods can also harm your teeth.

Be good to yourself. Choose complex carbohydrates instead of simple ones. Snack on popcorn, not biscuits. Start the day with a bowl of cereal instead of a muffin. You will feel the difference!

Getting it Right

What do athletes eat before a big event? They eat plenty of complex carbohydrates, such as pasta, for energy. Professional athletes say it is best to eat 1½ to 3 hours before you exercise and to limit sugar, caffeine, fats, and oil.

YOU CAN DO IT!

Make an olive oil bread dip

Instead of buttering your bread, try dipping it into flavoured olive oil. To make this recipe, you will need:

- *80ml extra virgin olive oil*
- *1 clove of garlic, crushed*
- *small handful of fresh basil leaves, finely chopped*
- *bread*

1. Mix the oil, garlic, and basil in a bowl.
2. Warm the bread, drizzle the oil over it, and eat. Yummy!

Choosing the right fats

The type of fat you eat also affects your health. Saturated fats and trans fats can cause heart disease, **diabetes**, and **obesity**. They are found in meat and dairy products and in **processed foods** such as margarine, crisps, and biscuits.

Moderate amounts of unsaturated fats help to prevent heart disease. You get them in some vegetable oils, nuts, and seeds.

To look and feel your best, eat lean meat, fish, and yoghurt, and drink low-fat milk instead of full-fat products. Substitute nuts or seeds for crisps.

Build your bones

You are building most of your bone strength now. For strong bones, girls aged 9–18 need about 1,300 milligrams (²⁄₃ teaspoon) of the nutrient calcium a day. Here's where to find it:

- milk
- yoghurt, frozen yoghurt
- ice cream
- broccoli, kale
- sardines
- cheese – including macaroni cheese, grilled cheese sandwiches, cheese pizza
- tofu
- orange juice fortified with calcium

Be sure to choose low-fat products, which have the added benefit of decreasing the fat in your diet.

Drink water!

Drinking water instead of soft drinks is a great idea. Water cleanses your body and keeps you healthy. You need about eight glasses a day. Get into the habit of carrying water with you. If you don't like drinking water, flavour it with a lemon slice or add a splash of fruit juice. Make water a regular part of your diet.

Satisfying your thirst with water helps your body to work properly and keeps your skin looking its best.

Getting the right amounts

Working out what and how much to eat doesn't have to be confusing. To feel your best, girls aged 9–18 need: 2–3 portions of dairy, 5 portions of fruit and vegetables, 170 grams of grains, and140 grams of meat, eggs, fish, or beans every day. Try keeping a food diary to see if you are getting all the foods you need each day.

Learning about labels

Food labels can help. They tell you the amount of nutrients in a serving of food and what is considered an appropriate serving. A label on a container of mixed nuts, for example, tells you that 30 nuts equals one serving. Check the label to see whether you are overeating or under-eating.

TIP

Don't skip breakfast. It gives you energy to start the day. If you don't like traditional breakfast foods, have a smoothie, last night's leftovers, a sandwich, or a bowl of soup instead.

The label also gives the number of **calories** in a serving. A moderately active teenage girl, weighing 45 kilograms needs about 2,200 calories a day. The more active you are, the more calories you burn.

For Best Before End, see top flap.
Nutrition: Typical average values

	Per 40g serving	Per 100g
Energy	597kJ/ 141kcal	1493kJ/ 353kcal
Protein	4.3g	10.7g
Carbohydrate (of which sugars	25.7g 6.3g	64.3g 15.9g)
Fat (of which saturates	2.4g 0.3g	5.9g 0.7g)
Fibre (of which soluble (of which insoluble	3.1g 0.9g 2.2g	7.7g 2.2g) 5.5g)
Sodium	0.07g	0.17g
Salt	0.17g	0.43g

This row shows how much energy (calories) the food contains per seving.

These rows show the amounts of individual nutrients, in grams, per serving.

10

Getting it Wrong

Looking and feeling healthy means eating well. There are signs to watch out for that show you are not eating properly. You may not be getting all the nutrients you need if you:

- feel tired all the time
- are irritable
- have thin hair
- have problem skin
- have fingernails that break easily.

Try adding more fruit to your diet – this will give your body a vitamin boost.

Eating out

Although you cannot usually check food labels at restaurants, you can still make the right choices. Keep the following in mind the next time you eat out:

- order a tomato or meat sauce, instead of a creamy sauce
- order a baked potato, not chips
- order a hamburger, not a bacon cheeseburger
- order roast, not fried, chicken.

What to look for

Some foods, such as cakes and sweets, contain lots of calories but few nutrients. Check to see that you are eating foods that are high in protein, fibre, vitamins, and minerals. Choose foods that are low in sugar and fats. You want unsaturated fats, not saturated or trans fats (see page 8).

Check the salt (also called sodium). Teenage girls need about 1,500 milligrams (¾ teaspoon) a day. Most processed foods are pre-salted, so avoid eating these if possible. Keep an eye on how much sodium you are eating – too much can cause **high blood pressure**. Taste your food before adding salt. Your food will be perfectly seasoned, and you will be healthier if you do.

DID YOU KNOW?

Plate size counts! Scientists have found that the larger a plate or bowl is, the more food a person eats. If you want to avoid overeating, use smaller plates and utensils.

FOOD, BODY IMAGE, AND EMOTIONS

Your body image is your impression of how your body looks. It is not always correct. Although your body may be strong and healthy, if you compare it to that of a celebrity or fashion model, you may have a negative body image.

Some models go to extremes to be thin. They do this in order to compete in a business in which looking a certain way is valued more than a person's health. Comparing yourself to these women is not realistic.

Concentrate on eating well and exercising regularly – make the most of what you have. Dress to emphasize your good features, greet others with a friendly smile, and celebrate the total person you are. Soon you will begin to see yourself more clearly.

If you suspect you have an eating disorder, get help. Talk to your parents, a school nurse or counsellor, or your doctor.

Think about a woman you admire. Do you admire her because she looks like a fashion model, or because of the kind of person she is?

Emotions and eating

Emotions can play a part in what and how much you eat. Feelings such as sadness, anger, loneliness, and stress can cause you to under-eat or overeat.

Emotional eating can lead to dangerous eating disorders such as obesity, in which people overeat. Other disorders include **bulimia**, in which people overeat then **purge**, and **anorexia**, in which people under-eat. All three disorders can cause serious health problems.

If emotions are causing you to under-eat, focus on what you like about yourself instead of your weight. Make a list of your good points. Check the list whenever you feel low. Remember that your body size is just a small part of what makes you an individual. There is a lot more to you than your weight. If emotions are causing you to overeat, substituting a healthy activity like walking or calling a friend can help to fill your emotional need.

• CHECKLIST •

How to spot the signs of anorexia or bulimia

You might have a problem if you:

- think you are overweight even if no one else does
- worry about your weight and what you eat all the time
- vomit, use laxatives, or do not eat when you are hungry in order to control your weight
- value yourself based on how thin you are.

Are you an emotional eater?

Emotional eaters eat in response to feelings instead of to hunger. You may be an emotional eater if you eat:

- to comfort yourself when you are sad, angry, upset, or lonely
- to reward yourself
- to fill a feeling of emptiness
- to calm down
- out of boredom.

MAINTAINING A BALANCE

You can eat healthily and still enjoy your favourite treats. Just don't eat treats instead of healthier food or in large quantities. If you love pizza, have a slice – but have a side salad instead of a second slice. Or try vegetable toppings instead of meat. That way, you will get plenty of vitamins and minerals.

Go ahead and have the enchiladas you love, but ask for a **starter** portion as your main course. Get a small order of chips instead of "super-sizing". Once you have learned about portion sizes, you will see it is easy to take care of yourself and enjoy your food.

Sharing a sweet dessert with a friend is fun, saves you money, and keeps you from eating too much sugar.

Getting it Right

Some healthy snack ideas:

- for a crunchy snack, try baby carrots
- for a cold and creamy snack, try low-fat frozen yoghurt
- for a different kind of snack, try rice cakes topped with peanut butter
- for a spicy snack, dust popcorn with chilli powder
- for a sweet snack, try fresh fruit.

Be adventurous

Try new foods! If you make eating an adventure, you will enjoy food for its taste rather than its quantity. You might find that you like sushi, which is full of nutrients. Top a baked potato with salsa or fat-free yoghurt instead of sour cream and butter. You can eat healthily without feeling hungry or unsatisfied. You will also feel great because you are getting plenty of nutrients.

Make trail mix

Trail mix makes a great high-energy snack. Use your favourite kinds of nuts, dried fruit, seeds, and wholegrain cereal. Be creative! To make this recipe, you will need:

- 100g almonds
- 100g shelled sunflower seeds
- 100g raisins
- 100g low-fat granola or wheat cereal
- 100g dried cranberries

1. Mix all the ingredients together in a bowl.
2. Store in sealed plastic bags.
3. Remember to take a small bag with you when you go out. You never know when you might get hungry!

ARE YOU A HEALTHY EATER?

1) **How often do you eat breakfast?**
   a) Never.
   b) At the weekend.
   c) Every day.

2) **How often do you drink water?**
   a) Rarely.
   b) Occasionally.
   c) Often.

3) **What is your favourite snack?**
   a) Sweets.
   b) Salted, buttered popcorn.
   c) Fruit.

4) **When do you usually eat?**
   a) When you're upset.
   b) When you're watching television.
   c) When you're hungry.

5) **Do you eat dairy products:**
   a) rarely?
   b) occasionally?
   c) often?

6) **For long-lasting energy, do you eat:**
   a) a slice of chocolate cake?
   b) a handful of nuts?
   c) pasta with vegetables?

Check page 50 to see if you are a healthy eater.

15

Glow With Fitness

Keeping fit is an important part of taking care of yourself. Adding fitness to your life improves your overall health, and has a positive effect on how you look and feel.

Going out for a jog with your friends lets you strengthen your body, enjoy the fresh air, and spend time with people you care about.

Make Fitness a Part of Your Life

Participating in physical activity does great things for your body. Physical activity strengthens your bones, joints, muscles, heart, and lungs. It also burns calories. If you eat more calories than your body uses for energy, your body stores the extra calories as fat. Being active burns fat and keeps you in shape.

There are lots of ways to add fitness to your daily life. Take the stairs rather than the lift. Ride your bike to school. Go for a walk after supper. Keeping fit does not need to be expensive or take a lot of time.

Fitness with friends

Make physical activity a social event. Going skating with a friend is a fun activity that keeps you both fit. Playing Frisbee or cycling with your family gives you quality time together and is good for everyone's health.

Fitness at home

There are lots of things you can do around the house to keep fit.

- Gardening: weeding and raking are excellent ways to burn calories.

- Cleaning the house: vacuuming and sweeping raise your heart rate and help keep you fit.

- Walking the dog, or a neighbour's dog, with a friend: a great way to exercise, catch up with your friend, or help a neighbour.

- Playing football or chase with your brother or sister: good ways to get exercise and connect with loved ones.

FITNESS AND BODY SHAPE

Every woman's body is shaped differently. The **genes** you inherit determine your body shape. Body shapes are described as apple, pear, hourglass, or ruler.

APPLE
If you have an apple shape, you have small hips and a round stomach.

PEAR
If you are pear-shaped, your hips are wide and your chest and shoulders are narrow.

HOURGLASS
Hourglasses have small waists with fairly equally sized tops and bottoms.

RULER
Rulers have straight bodies with few curves.

Exercises, such as push-ups, sit-ups, pull-ups, and squats, strengthen your body. They don't give you bulging muscles, but they do tone and shape you.

Enhancing your shape

You cannot change your body shape. But you can strengthen and **enhance** it with physical activity.

- Activities that strengthen your lower body, such as skating, walking uphill, skiing, and skipping, make an apple-shaped body appear more balanced.

- Upper-body activities such as pull-ups, push-ups, rowing, and swimming add balance to a pear's body.

- Belly dancing and hula dancing or twirling a hoop around your waist can add curves to a ruler-shaped body.

- Activities such as jogging and dancing keep an hourglass-shaped body **toned**.

All body shapes are beautiful. Be proud of your body and what it can do. Keeping fit is about feeling good from the inside out.

How much energy are you burning?

It is good to know how much energy, in the form of calories, you are using up. This list tells you how many calories a girl weighing 45 kilograms could burn doing the following activities for 30 minutes.

- Stretching, yoga: 60 calories
- Bowling, volleyball: 71 calories
- Gymnastics, walking: 95 calories
- Dancing: 114 calories
- Skateboarding: 119 calories
- Horse riding: 155 calories
- Jogging, tennis, swimming, football: 167 calories
- Lacrosse: 191 calories
- Skipping, karate: 238 calories
- Skating: 286 calories
- Running: 357 calories

DID YOU KNOW?

Your body mass index (BMI) is a way to calculate whether your weight is in the healthy range for your height. Why don't you give it a try?

1. Multiply your height in metres by itself.

2. Divide your weight in kilograms by the number you got in step 1.

Now take a look at your results:

- If your BMI is under 19, you may be underweight.

- If your BMI is between 19 and 25, you are probably at a healthy weight.

- If your BMI is over 25, you may be overweight.

Getting it Right

Although knowing your BMI is helpful, it is only part of calculating your overall health. If you are worried that you may be overweight or underweight, talk to an adult such as your school nurse, a parent or guardian, or a doctor. These people will be able to give you good advice about things you can do to improve your overall health and fitness.

WHAT'S RIGHT FOR YOU?

Being physically active can be lots of fun. The key is finding activities that are right for you.

Joining in

If you like being part of a group, join a sports team. You don't need to be a star athlete to join, as long as you are willing to be a team player. Or enrol in an exercise class. Community centres and health clubs offer classes such as salsa, yoga, and aerobics. Learning a martial art, such as kickboxing, will help to **empower** you. Ballet can make you more graceful.

Getting it Right

Warming up and cooling down before and after you exercise helps to prevent injuries. Warm up by stretching. Do side bends, knee lifts, and calf stretches. Get your heart rate up by fast walking or jogging on the spot. Cool down with stretches and slow walking.

Gymnastics is an activity you can do alone or in a group. It strengthens, tones, and stretches the body.

Strengthen your abs

Try doing "X-crunches" to strengthen your **abdominal muscles**.

1. Lie on your back with your knees bent and your feet on the floor. Cross you arms on your chest in an "X".

2. Use your stomach muscles to lift your upper body, then lower it.

You may not be able to lift your body much at first. The more you practise, the better you will get. Start off with five, then increase by five as you find they get easier to do. Remember that the quality of the "crunch" is as important as the quantity. Do not swing, jerk, or tug on your neck.

Time alone or time with a friend

If you need some time alone, walking, cycling, kite flying, and jogging are great solo activities. Or maybe exercise will allow you to spend time with a friend. Playing tennis or badminton are just two of the ways you can be active with a mate.

Be realistic

Try different activities until you find some you enjoy. If an activity makes you feel good, it is right for you – but be practical. For example, if you live in the tropics, snowboarding isn't a good option, but surfing is. Look at your budget, too. If it is limited, activities that require expensive equipment, such as scuba diving, might not be suitable. Try a similar but less pricey alternative, like swimming. Whatever you choose, once you get moving you'll be surprised how great you feel.

When exercising: **TIP**

- comfortable clothes and athletic shoes with rubber soles are ideal
- a one-piece swimsuit is best for swimming
- wear sunglasses outdoors to protect your eyes
- wear a cap or a headband to keep your hair off your face
- safety gear, such as a cycle helmet, is essential.

PHYSICAL ACTIVITY AND EMOTIONS

Physical activity has a positive effect on your emotions. It causes the body to release chemicals called endorphins that relieve stress and improve your mood.

Physical activity can also boost your self-confidence, especially if you set physical goals and achieve them. Start with a small goal and work your way up. If you want to run a 5-kilometre race, your first goal might be to run 1 kilometre. When you can do that, add another kilometre, and so on. You will soon be ready for the race and proud of what you can do!

Physical activity and friendship

Being physically active can also help you make new friends. Being a member of a team or an exercise class brings you together with people with whom you share a common interest. Try out for the football or netball team , or join a judo club. You can even start your own club. How about a Saturday cycling or walking club?

But remember that you do not have to rely on teams and classes, other people, or expensive equipment to keep fit. You can be active whenever the chance arises. You will feel better physically and emotionally if you do.

Team mates share a common goal and have fun together. It is no wonder that they often become close friends.

DID YOU KNOW?

Yoga is an ancient form of exercise that can strengthen your muscles, improve your flexibility, and relax you. You can learn yoga from a book or DVD, or you can join a class. While practising yoga, you slowly move your body through a variety of poses.

HOW ACTIVE ARE YOU?

1) **Your best friend asks you to join a salsa dancing class with her. Do you:**
   a) sign up, too?
   b) stay at home and listen to music?
   c) prefer window shopping?

2) **The dentist's office is on the third floor. Do you:**
   a) take the stairs?
   b) wait for the lift?
   c) take the lift up and walk down the stairs?

3) **Your class mates are sponsoring a charity run. Do you:**
   a) enter it and run?
   b) watch from the sidelines?
   c) walk around the course?

4) **At the beach do you:**
   a) swim, swim, swim?
   b) relax under an umbrella?
   c) stroll along the shore?

5) **You wake up early. Do you:**
   a) decide to walk to school?
   b) watch some morning television?
   c) tidy your bedroom?

7) **Your PE teacher brings out the trampoline. Do you:**
   a) make sure you're first in line to get on and have a go?
   b) hide in the changing room?
   c) jump once then get off?

Check page 50 to see how active you are.

SLEEP: YOUR SECRET WEAPON

To feel your best, you need 7–9 hours of sleep each night. While you sleep, your body **restores** itself. If you do not get enough, you are more likely to get ill, feel tired and irritable, and have trouble thinking clearly. Lack of sleep can also damage your appearance – giving you dull skin and dark circles under your eyes.

TIPS FOR A GOOD NIGHT'S SLEEP

If you want to look and feel your best, take steps to make sure you are getting enough sleep. Exercise during the day – it helps you sleep better. Record late-night films instead of watching them. Turn off your computer at a reasonable hour. Don't make phone calls after a certain time.

Before you go to bed, do not:
- eat a big meal
- watch a scary film
- listen to loud, stimulating music
- wait until the last minute to do homework or revision
- think about your problems
- drink or eat foods that contain caffeine such as tea, coffee, coke, or chocolate.

Bedtime rituals

Create a bedtime routine, such as brushing your teeth, reading a bit, and then turning out the light. Doing the same thing each night tells your body it is time to sleep. Set aside time to relax before bedtime as part of your routine. Try having a warm bath or listening to soothing music.

Take charge of how much sleep you get. Set your bedtime at a reasonable hour, and make it the same every night.

Getting it Right

Drinking a cup of warm milk, camomile or peppermint tea 15 minutes before going to bed can help you fall asleep. They contain chemicals that relax your body and mind.

Keeping your bedroom cool, quiet, and dark helps you to sleep better. Lower the heat, draw the curtains, and block out outside noise with earplugs.

Getting it
Wrong

Sleeping in late at the weekend is not a good idea. It can upset your body's natural rhythm and make you less alert on Monday morning. If you are really tired, you can always lie down for a rest during the weekend to restore yourself.

DID YOU KNOW?

Most teenagers do not get enough sleep, and the effects can be serious. Many pupils fall asleep in class occasionally. Lack of sleep makes it difficult to concentrate. This can be particularly dangerous if you drive a car, because drivers need to be alert in order to prevent accidents.

Body Basics

Puberty is the process of changing from a child to an adult. It causes many changes in young people's bodies, some of which may make you feel uncomfortable, such as **acne** and body odour. You can manage these changes in a positive way. When you do, you will feel better about yourself.

GAIN CONTROL

It takes time to get used to what is happening to you. The changes in your body don't change who you are. Don't worry about the spot on your forehead. Focus on your good points. Identify one thing you like about yourself every day and emphasize it. Put something pretty in your hair. Wear rings on your nicely shaped fingers. If you focus on your good points, so will other people.

Don't compare yourself to your friends. Everyone's body changes at its own rate. If you have questions, talk to a trusted older woman, such as your mother, aunt, or teacher.

Personal hygiene

Adapt your personal **hygiene** routine to deal with the changes in your body. To eliminate unpleasant body odour caused by **perspiration**, have a shower after exercising. Use soap and underarm deodorant. Prevent smelly feet by changing your socks often and sprinkling baby powder in your shoes.

YOU CAN DO IT!

Treat yourself to a spa bath

A warm bath cleanses you, keeps you smelling sweet, and relaxes you. Try adding some homemade bath salts for a spa experience. To create your own spa bath, you will need:

- *100g Epsom salts (magnesium sulfate)*
- *1 tablespoon baking soda*
- *1 teaspoon fragrance, such as lemon juice or vanilla*

1. Mix all the ingredients together.
2. Pour the mixture into the bath as it fills with warm water. Enjoy!

If you have any allergies or sensitive skin, adding a fragrance may not be for you.

Germs are spread when, for example, someone with a cold touches an object such as a doorknob. When you touch that object, the germs spread to you. Washing your hands for 30 seconds gets rid of germs. If you cannot get to a sink to wash your hands, carry anti-bacterial gel, which kills **bacteria** on contact. Use it before you eat a meal or snack.

Smile

Practise good dental hygiene to keep your teeth clean and your breath fresh. Carry floss and a toothbrush in your bag, to use after eating. Rinse with mouthwash in the morning and evening. Avoid coke, coffee, and some teas, which can stain your teeth. Visit your dentist regularly to keep your teeth healthy. These little things can make a big difference to how you look and feel.

If you wear braces, caring for your teeth needs special attention. Brush between the wires and your gums. Use a toothpick to loosen stubborn bits of food.

YOUR SKIN TYPE

During puberty your body produces excess oil. The oil, along with bacteria and dead skin, can get trapped in your **pores**. This is what causes acne.

Having a daily skin care routine can help keep your skin healthy. Try to wash your face several times a day with warm water and a mild soap. Choose a soap that is right for your skin type.

Your skin may be oily, dry, normal, or a combination. If your skin feels tight and is flaky after washing, it is dry. If it is shiny or feels greasy, it is oily. If it is neither oily nor dry, it is considered normal. And if it is dry in some places and oily in others, it is combination skin. Most teenagers have oily or combination skin.

Caring for your skin

Treat your skin gently. Use cotton wool pads or your fingers (which, of course, you have washed first) and soap to cleanse your face. After washing, rinse your face with cool water. Pat it dry with a clean towel. Although it is tempting, don't squeeze spots! It only makes your skin red and swollen.

Getting it Right

Here are some steps you can take to help avoid spots and keep your skin looking great:

- If your hair is oily, keep it off your face.
- Keep your hands off your face.
- Don't rest your chin in your hands.
- Drink plenty of water.
- Avoid oil-based make-up.

Sun safety

Acne isn't the only problem for your skin – the Sun can be dangerous. Don't forget to apply suncream every day before you go outside. It helps to prevent wrinkles and it protects you against skin cancer. Choose non-oil-based suncream with **SPF**15 or higher. If you want to look tanned, try a self-tanning lotion.

Make a face mask

Try making a mask that is good for oily skin. To make this you will need:

- *100g strawberries*
- *1 tablespoon cornstarch*

1. Mash the ingredients together to form a paste.
2. Gently rub the paste onto your face, but keep it away from your eyes.
3. Leave it on for 20 minutes, then rinse with cool water.

If you have any allergies or sensitive skin, a face mask may not be for you.

Your fridge is full of ingredients for a face mask. Try mashed avocado for dry skin, mashed kiwi for oily skin, or egg white and cooked oatmeal for combination skin. You can also try using over-the-counter products made for skin that tends to get spots. Or if you have a particularly bad case of acne, your doctor can prescribe special lotions and drugs.

TIP

You might want to try to **exfoliate** or to use a face mask once a week. This will remove dead skin that clogs your pores. A mask also soothes your skin.

DEVELOPING BREASTS

The most visible change in your body is the development of your breasts. At first they may be uneven. Don't worry – this is often only temporary. Don't worry about their size, either. There is no way to predict a young woman's final breast size.

Measuring up

As your breasts develop, you may want to start wearing a bra. When to start is a personal decision. When you shop for a bra, choose one that feels comfortable and fits well. Let the saleswoman measure you to find out your bra size. It will have a number and a letter. The number measures the size of your back and chest. The letter measures the cup. A bra that fits well should not cut into your skin. If it does, the number size is too small. If it is loose, the number size is too large. Try the next letter size up if your breasts bulge out of the cups. Drop down a letter size if your breasts do not fill the cups.

Choosing the right bra

Bras are made for different purposes.
- A sports bra keeps your breasts stable while you exercise. Wearing a sports bra provides almost twice as much support as a regular bra. When you try on a new sports bra, jump or jog on the spot to test its support.
- A padded bra makes your breasts look bigger.

YOU CAN DO IT!

Give yourself a breast examination

It is important to examine your breasts for suspicious lumps that could be a sign of breast cancer. Do this once a month, a few days after your period ends.
Follow these steps:

1. Lie down, with your right hand behind your head.

2. Using your fingers, move your left hand in an up and down pattern around your right breast.

3. Switch hand positions and repeat the examination with your right hand on your left breast.

If you feel any hard lumps, don't worry, but do tell an adult or your doctor.

- A minimizing bra makes your breasts look smaller.
- An underwired bra lifts your breasts.
- A convertible bra lets you remove or change the position of the straps.

DID YOU KNOW?

The clothes you wear can make your breasts look bigger or smaller.

- If you want to make your breasts look bigger, choose tops with chest pockets, ruffles, embroidery, bright colours, or large prints.
- If you want to make your breasts look smaller, choose tops with a V-neck or boat neck, solid colours, vertical stripes, or a loose fit.

Bra shopping is one of the special things that only girls get to enjoy. Don't worry if you find the experience uncomfortable or embarrassing. These feelings are normal.

YOUR HAIR

Your hair is something to be proud of. Taking care of it keeps it looking great.

Caring for your hair

Washing your hair regularly is the first step. Use a shampoo made specifically for your hair type – oily, dry, or normal. Wash oily hair every day and other hair types a few times a week. If you are unsure of your hair type, ask your hairdresser.

Different hair, different care

Depending on your hair type, you might try a volumizing shampoo to add fullness or a shampoo formulated to control frizz and seal split ends. Anti-dandruff shampoo fights dandruff, the flaky white specks caused by dead skin.

Applying a conditioner after shampooing adds moisture to your hair. It is especially important if you use styling products such as gel and hairspray, or styling tools like hot rollers, a blow dryer, or a curling iron, which dry out your hair.

Keep it to yourself

Don't share your styling tools with anyone else. This can spread head lice, tiny insects that can attach to your hair or scalp.

YOU CAN DO IT!

Make a herbal hair conditioner

Different herbs give different results. For example, rosemary controls dandruff, sage is good for oily hair, and camomile adds shine. To make your own herbal hair conditioner, you will need:

- *1 teaspoon of a herb suitable for your hair*
- *250ml hot water*

1. Put the herbs in a tea infuser. (This is the device in which you place tea leaves when you make tea.)
2. Put the infuser in the hot water and leave it there until the water cools.
3. Pour the cooled herbal tea over your freshly washed hair. Leave it on for five minutes, then rinse.

If you have any allergies or sensitive skin, a herbal conditioner may not be for you.

The perfect hairstyle

You won't need to use as many hair tools or products if you choose a hairstyle that complements your hair texture. If your hair is curly or wavy, a layered hairstyle will add volume. If it is straight, a blunt cut will show off your sleek hair. Whatever the texture and length of your hair, to keep it looking neat and to combat split ends, get it trimmed every four to six weeks. A good haircut can work wonders.

Your face shape also affects which hairstyle is best for you. To find out the shape of your face, compare the width of your forehead, jaw, and cheeks. Then, select a hairstyle that complements you – a few are outlined below!

It is fun to try new hairstyles. Add sparkly clips; pin a flower behind your ear; part your hair on the opposite side; or pull it back with a headband.

Hair styles for different face shapes		
Face shape	**Characteristics**	**Hairstyle tips**
Round	Full cheeks, few angles.	Soft layers that fall just below the chin, avoid a straight fringe.
Heart	Wide forehead, narrow, pointy chin.	Side-swept fringe, hair that falls below your jaw.
Square	Wide forehead, straight, strong jaw.	Layered cuts, choppy ends.
Rectangle	Long, narrow face, straight forehead and jaw.	Chin-length bob with a fringe, avoid long hair.
Oval	Egg-shaped face.	All styles flatter ovals; try layers around your face.

MENSTRUATION

Part of becoming a woman is **menstruation**, or getting your period. Most women get their period about every 28 days, and it lasts for two to seven days. At first, your cycle may be irregular. Once it becomes regular, keeping track of it on a calendar helps you to manage it. A few days before you expect your period, slip a tampon or sanitary pad in your school locker and another in your bag. That way, no matter where you are, your period won't catch you by surprise.

Managing your period

It is normal to lose about 10 teaspoons of blood during a typical period. You will probably bleed more in the first few days than the last few. Using higher absorbency pads or tampons on your heavier days, and lower absorbency ones on your lighter days, helps you to feel more comfortable and confident. Changing your tampon or pad every few hours also helps. It prevents unpleasant odours and leakage, and protects you from **toxic shock syndrome**.

If you get pains before or during your period, take steps to ease them. A warm bath, a heating pad on your stomach, or a painkiller such as ibuprofen all help. Exercising also relieves period pains, while caffeine and fried food can worsen them.

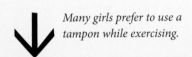

Many girls prefer to use a tampon while exercising.

DID YOU KNOW?

If you feel moody, tired, irritable, bloated, have sore breasts, and/or cry more easily a few days before your period, you may have a condition known as *premenstrual tension*, or "PMT".

Getting it Right

Don't let PMT get the better of you.

• Drink plenty of water

• Wear a supportive bra

• Avoid caffeine

• Exercise gently

• Eat a balanced diet

• Get plenty of sleep

• Take time to relax

HOW WELL DO YOU CARE FOR YOUR BODY?

1) **Do you brush and floss your teeth:**
   a) after every meal?
   b) morning and evening?
   c) Floss? What's that?

2) **Do you use suncream:**
   a) every day?
   b) sometimes?
   c) never?

3) **Do you shower or bathe:**
   a) daily and after you exercise?
   b) daily?
   c) once a week?

4) **Do you have your hair cut:**
   a) often?
   b) twice a year?
   c) never — you're letting it grow?

5) **To ease PMT, do you:**
   a) exercise, eat well, and get plenty of sleep?
   b) take painkillers, but don't exercise?
   c) drink coffee?

Check page 50 to see how well you take care of your body.

ACCEPT YOURSELF AND OTHERS

Your preteen and teenage years are an emotional time. Learning to deal with your emotions in a positive way can help you to feel great, or at least to understand your many and different emotions.

CHANGING HORMONES

Puberty causes chemicals in your body called **hormones** to rise and fall. This causes you to feel more emotions – and to feel them more intensely – than at any other time in your life. It is no wonder that a television commercial can bring tears to your eyes, or an innocent comment from a classmate can make you want to transfer to a new school.

Keep in mind that you are extremely sensitive at the moment. Take a deep breath and step away from a situation before you react. It is OK to be angry when your sister borrows your clothes without asking. Shouting at her might make you feel better for a moment, but you will probably regret your behaviour later. Your reaction should be something that you can be proud of, not something you will regret.

Dealing with your emotions

When you feel negative emotions are taking over:

- count to 10 before you react
- walk away from the situation
- recite a silent poem
- listen to music
- watch a silly film
- think about something that makes you happy.

Keeping a diary can also help you sort out your worries and problems. Writing things down helps you gain a better understanding of what is bothering you and why.

If you cannot seem to get control, talk to a trusted older person, such as a family member, teacher, or school counsellor. These people can help you come to terms with how you are feeling and give advice that may help put you back in charge of your emotions.

Sometimes the best way to cope with negative emotions is to get a change of scenery. Go for a walk or spend some time in the library.

Getting it
Right

If you are not comfortable talking to a family member about your problems, your school counsellor, a social worker, or a psychologist are all good people to turn to. These people are trained to listen without judging you. They can give you tips on how to cope, can talk to your parents for you, and can arrange further help, if necessary.

Getting it
Wrong

Using drugs or alcohol to mask your problems is unwise. They reduce your ability to think clearly, making you more likely to say or do something you will regret. Drugs and alcohol also damage your health. Talk to an adult if you are tempted to use them.

ESTABLISHING YOUR IDENTITY

Part of growing up is establishing your own identity. Finding out who you are can be confusing, but also fun. Think about what is important to you. If you had time to do only one hobby, or to study only one subject at school, what would you choose? Follow your heart. If you love everything about cars, sign up for a mechanics class – even if you are the only girl!

Find a role model or **mentor** – someone you admire and can learn from. For instance, if you admire your English teacher because she treats everyone with respect and never goes back on her word, try doing the same. Examine people's good points. Do they look you in the eye and greet you with a smile? Adopting these characteristics might help you clarify the identity you want for yourself.

Getting it Right

If you want your parents to treat you as if you are growing up, here are some ways to earn their trust:

- do your chores and homework without being reminded
- respect your **curfew**
- work hard
- take responsibility for your actions.

Who are you?

Below is a list of character traits. Choose the ones most important to you, and try to incorporate them into your life.

How actions influence character	
Character trait	**Action**
Friendly	Greet everyone, ask how they are, and listen to their answers.
Clever	Read, work hard, and perhaps help a younger child.
Trustworthy	Keep secrets and don't gossip.
Imaginative	Draw, write, sew, or build something original.
Caring	Do volunteer work.
Generous	Organise a cake or secondhand clothes sale.
Confident	Walk with your head held high, and put up your hand in lessons.

Becoming independent

Establishing your identity can sometimes lead to family tensions. You may want to be more independent and make your own decisions, but your parents may not think you are ready. Try to compromise. Talk to your parents without shouting. Listen to their opinions. Let your actions prove to them that they can trust you.

Remember that growing up is a gradual process. Your parents want to help you. It is OK to need their support.

Babysitting is a good way to show your parents you are growing up. Knowing that you can care for a young child will help your parents to trust you more, because it requires a great deal of responsibility.

Your self-esteem

All the changes you are going through can make you feel self-conscious and lower your **self-esteem**. Just as you can strengthen your physical self by eating well, exercising, and getting enough sleep, you can take steps to strengthen your emotional self by boosting your self-esteem.

Focus on your good points. List them in your diary. Think in terms of what you can do, rather than what you can't do. Remember that no one is perfect. Just because you did badly in a school test does not mean you are a failure. Instead of thinking about what you did wrong, concentrate on how you can do better next time. Make a plan and act on it.

DID YOU KNOW?

Recent research has shown that in the first years of primary school plenty of girls will say they are good at many things. When the girls reach the top of primary school, fewer will say this. When the girls reach secondary school, even fewer will say it. Although the girls' abilities do not decrease as they get older, their self-esteem does. Don't let this happen to you!

Boost your confidence

Your attitude is everything. Behave as if you are confident, even if you don't feel it. Stand up straight. Hold your head high. Look directly at people. Say hello. Share a smile. Soon you will start believing in yourself, and others will follow. Remember that no matter how self-conscious you feel, you are not alone. Your **peers** are all going through the same things. Although it might be hard to believe, even the most popular girl in your class feels insecure sometimes.

TIP

- Mentally tell yourself that you are important.
- Do one thing every day that you can be proud of.
- Get involved in an activity that focuses on others.
- Make a special effort to look your best.
- Set a goal and work to achieve it.

It takes confidence to give a presentation. To make it easier, be prepared. Practise beforehand. Take a deep breath. Look straight ahead. Speak loudly and clearly.

Getting it **Right**

Good posture makes you look thinner, taller, stronger, and more confident. Stand in front of a mirror and check your posture. From the side, your hips, shoulders, and ears should be in line. Your upper back and shoulders should be straight, not slouched or rounded. Your head should be held high. Be aware of your posture. Soon standing tall will be second nature to you!

YOU AND YOUR FRIENDS

As you become more independent and struggle with your identity, having friends becomes more important. Sharing feelings helps you to feel normal and secure.

Friendships at this time of life can be challenging. As you start establishing your identity, your interests may become different from your friends' interests. It is normal to feel sad if this happens. If you no longer have much in common, you can keep your old friends, but making new friends with common interests is good, too.

Getting it Right

Your friends are individuals – don't expect them to agree with everything you say. Unless what you disagree about affects your health or safety, you can disagree and still be friends. Don't take differences of opinion personally. The world would be a boring place if everyone was the same.

Good friends are there for each other, no matter what. They share each other's happiness and sadness. They know they can count on each other.

Meeting new people

Making new friends can be difficult, especially if you are shy. Take a deep breath and make the first move. You are not the only one who feels insecure. Talk to your classmates. Start a conversation about a school project, an upcoming event, or the school food. If someone seems interesting, invite them to do something with you.

Join a club or a youth group. Do volunteer work. If you get involved in something that interests you, you will meet people like you. Even if they don't go to your school, you can be friends with them.

Being a good friend

It is OK to have different groups of friends. And it is OK for your best friend to have other friends, too. You don't have to share everything to be friends. Real friendships involve give and take. Although you can "take" comfort and companionship from your friends, you also have to "give" them your understanding and trust in order to form special relationships. Treat your friends the way you want to be treated, and expect the same in return.

Getting it Wrong

Sometimes girls gossip just to fit in. Gossip is hurtful. Think about how it makes you feel when you are the subject of gossip. You don't like being talked about, and neither do others. Treat everyone with respect. If you do, you will be liked and respected, too.

Good friends have a number of certain qualities. They:

- aren't jealous of each other
- make time for each other
- don't gossip or tell lies about each other
- encourage each other
- keep each other's secrets (unless the secret can injure a friend's health)
- laugh with, not at, each other.

Cliques

Cliques are groups of people who hang around together. Some cliques are composed of loyal friends who are accepting of others. Other cliques are based on shallow friendships and are characterised by members being mean to non-members. These cliques often have a leader who tells the members what they must do to fit in.

Be yourself

You may think being part of such a clique will raise your social standing. But you should be accepted for who you are, not for someone you pretend to be. If you get involved in activities that interest you, you will find friends who share your values and accept the real you.

If you are a member of a clique, don't give up your other activities because of the clique. Encourage those within your group to be accepting of others, and speak out if you feel your friends are being mean to non-members. Other clique members may feel the same way, but are afraid to speak up. If they don't have a problem with this sort of behaviour, you might want to think about whether they are the kind of people you want to be friends with.

Peer pressure

Clique leaders are not the only ones telling their peers how to act. Your friends and schoolmates may pressure you to make decisions you are not comfortable with. This is known as **peer pressure**. Although it may be easier to go along with what others think or do, part of establishing your identity is doing what you think is right.

It takes courage to resist peer pressure. Here are some ways to help you cope:

* choose friends who share your values
* avoid people who pressure you
* avoid situations that present serious problems or dangerous choices
* say "No, thank you," and walk away from a tough situation
* think about the consequences before you act
* pay attention to your feelings
* don't do anything you are uncomfortable with
* remember to be assertive
* be true to yourself.

It may not be easy to resist peer pressure, but you will feel better about yourself if you do. If the pressure is too much for you, talk to a teacher, counsellor, parent, or other trusted adult. These people can help.

Getting it
Right

It is hard to be a stranger.
If a new person joins your
class, welcome them. Show
them around, introduce them
to your friends, and invite
them to spend time with you.
Your actions will mark you
as a leader as well as a kind,
caring, friendly person. You
will feel good about yourself,
and you may be rewarded
with a new friend!

*Many teens start smoking
because of peer pressure. Don't
let peer pressure make you do
something you will regret.*

Bullies and you

Bullies are people who pick on others to make themselves feel powerful. Bullies may tease you, spread rumours about you, or make you feel unsafe. They may use the Internet to bother you. Some bullies come from abusive families, where they learn bullying behaviour. If you are being bullied, it doesn't mean there is something wrong with you. The problem lies with the bully. It is not your fault, and you should not be embarrassed about it.

Don't suffer in silence! Tell someone in charge, like a parent, teacher, or head teacher, about what is going on. Bullies usually stop once an adult gets involved.

Coping with prejudice

Prejudice can also cause you to be mistreated. Prejudiced people make negative judgements about others without getting to know them, sometimes based on issues such as race or religion.

If you are the victim of prejudice, don't be ashamed of who you are. Let others get to know you. Ask a teacher to help you give a presentation about whatever it is that makes you different – the country you come from, your religion, or your disability. If others learn more about you, they will be less likely to be prejudiced.

Getting it Right

When dealing with a bully:

- tell an adult
- act brave – bullies pick on people they think will be scared of them
- avoid being alone – bullies don't usually attack groups,
- avoid the bully
- don't show your feelings – bullies want a reaction
- walk away
- report criminal behaviour to the police.

TIP

If you see prejudice, help to end it. Get to know someone whose background is different from yours. Volunteer to help a foreign student learn English. Read books and watch films about different cultures.

Friendship isn't about race or religion. It is about the person inside. Be open-minded when meeting new people – you might be surprised by how much you have in common.

HOW DO YOU HANDLE YOUR EMOTIONS?

1) **You get a "D" in a test. Do you:**
   a) cry hysterically?
   b) work harder?
   c) feel like a failure?

2) **Your best friend goes shopping with someone else. Do you:**
   a) never speak to her again?
   b) go for a jog with another friend?
   c) sulk?

3) **You spill milk all over yourself during lunch. Do you:**
   a) hide in the bathroom?
   b) laugh and clean it off the best you can?
   c) insist your mother brings you clean clothes?

4) **A mean girl makes fun of your clothes. Do you:**
   a) start an ugly rumour about her?
   b) shrug it off — what does she know?
   c) never wear those clothes again?

5) **Your team loses a big match. Do you:**
   a) shout at your team mates for playing badly?
   b) plan an extra practice so you do better next time?
   c) blame yourself?

Check page 50 to see how well you handle your emotions.

Believe, Dream, Plan, And Achieve!

No one can deny that becoming a young woman is challenging. It is also wonderful and fun.

Believe

By making well-informed, safe choices, you can take control. Be true to yourself by not letting others pressure you to do things you are not comfortable with. Care for your health and your body by eating well, exercising, getting plenty of sleep, practising good hygiene, and getting help from an adult when you need it. Think about others, and treat them the way you want to be treated.

Dream

Allow yourself to dream. Think about what you want to do today, tomorrow, and in the distant future. Set yourself goals and decide on an action plan. Begin a skin care routine if you want healthier-looking skin. Work hard in science lessons and volunteer in a hospital if you dream of being a doctor.

Plan

Setting yourself goals and working towards them is the difference between wishing for something and making it happen.

Achieve

Let your inner beauty shine through. Be happy and confident inside – this will make you look good on the outside, too.

• CHECKLIST •

Some tips on setting goals and getting started with planning.

- Think about what is important to you.
- Prioritise – decide what you want to achieve the most.
- Write down your goal.
- Break your goal down into manageable parts. What do you want to achieve every day, week, or month?
- Decide on a plan of action.
- Keep track of your successes.
- When you reach your goal, celebrate!

Make a happiness diary
Record little things that make you happy in a "happiness diary". It will help you to appreciate all the joy in your life. To make your diary, you will need:

- *a notebook*
- *a pen*

1. Every day write down at least one thing that made you happy. It can be anything – the scent of newly-mown grass, a good result, or your grandmother's smile.
2. When you are feeling sad, read your diary.
3. You can draw in your diary and put in pictures of people or things that make you happy. For extra fun, decorate the cover with pictures, glitter, feathers – whatever makes you feel good!

TIP

You should always want to do your best. But no one is perfect. Sometimes other people will do better than you. It is OK to make mistakes or to take part in an activity where you are not the star.

If you want to do well and go to university, start studying now. Only you can make it happen!

Quiz Results

QUIZ

ARE YOU A HEALTHY EATER?
For page 15

If you answered mostly:

a) S.O.S. You need a diet makeover! Start with small changes like eating fewer sweets.

b) You're on the right track. But you could do better. Eat a variety of foods.

c) Congratulations — when it comes to healthy eating, you're a genius!

QUIZ

HOW WELL DO YOU CARE FOR YOUR BODY?
For page 35

If you answered mostly:

a) You've got it right. You respect your body and take good care of it!

b) You take care of your body when you have the time. Make more time for yourself. You and your body deserve the best!

c) You are not taking care of yourself. Put your health first.

QUIZ

HOW ACTIVE ARE YOU?
For page 23

Give yourself two points for each "a" answer, zero for each "b" answer, and one point for each "c" answer.

- 0–4 points: Get off that couch! Add physical activity to your life. When you see what your body can do, you'll be pleased.

- 5–9 points: You've got the right idea. Challenge yourself to do more!

- 10–12 points: You get the gold medal for being active!

QUIZ

HOW DO YOU HANDLE YOUR EMOTIONS?
For page 47

If you answered mostly:

a) There's too much drama in your life! Take a deep breath and think before you react.

b) You're one cool cookie. You handle your emotions very well and still manage to be considerate of others. Congratulations!

c) Your emotions rule. Try to calm down and believe in yourself.

20 Things To Remember

1 Eat fresh foods that are naturally colourful as they often contain the most vitamins and minerals.

2 Drink eight glasses of water every day. It helps you feel better and is essential for healthy looking skin.

3 Incorporate fitness into your daily life. Do things you enjoy – fitness should be fun!

4 Instead of worrying about how your body looks, be proud of what your body can do.

5 Follow a sleep routine. Looking your best is hard if you do not get enough sleep, as it allows your skin to repair itself.

6 After eating, floss and brush your teeth, and freshen your breath with mouthwash.

7 Treat your skin gently. Follow a skin care routine and don't squeeze your spots!

8 Use suncream throughout the year. Apply it to every part of your skin that is exposed to the Sun.

9 Choose a hairstyle suitable for your hair texture and face shape. This will help you avoid overusing styling products that can damage your hair.

10 Keep track of your period on a calendar and carry a tampon or pad with you when your period is due.

11 Change tampons every four to eight hours.

12 Take a deep breath before reacting to an upsetting situation. If you are very upset, walk away.

13 Keeping a diary can help you sort out your feelings. Write about your problems, your feelings, your strengths, and things that make you happy.

14 Talk to a trusted adult about your problems – your parents, older relatives, teachers, a guidance counsellor, or the school nurse.

15 Emphasise your strengths. When you draw attention to your good points, others will notice them.

16 Don't compare yourself to others – no one is perfect. Be happy with who you are.

17 Treat others the way you want to be treated.

18 Don't change yourself, or do things you will regret, just to fit in. You do not have to meet someone else's standards, so choose friends who share your values.

19 Celebrate your uniqueness and take pride in who you are. Our differences make the world interesting and life fun.

20 Set goals for yourself and rejoice when you achieve them.

FURTHER INFORMATION

WEBSITES

www.teenagehealthfreak.org
A great site with advice and information on bullying, body change, alcohol, drugs, moods, and much more.

www.nhs.uk/Livewell/teengirls/Pages/Teengirlshome.aspx
This part of the National Health Service website has information on all aspects of teenage health for girls.

www.teenissues.co.uk
This excellent site has more than 120 articles on all aspects of teenage life.

BOOKS

Fab Girl's Guide to Getting Your Questions Answered (Discovery Girls, 2007)

Fabulous Hair, Maria Neuman (Dorling Kindersley, 2006)

Food for Feeling Healthy, Carol Ballard (Heinemann Library, 2007)

Girls Speak Out: Finding Your True Self, Andrea Johnston (Celestial Arts, 2005)

The Diary of a Teenage Health Freak, Aidan Macfarlane, Ann McPherson and John Astrop (Oxford University Press, 2002)

What's Happening to My Body?, Lynda Madaras (Newmarket Press, 2008)

Why Should I Wash My Hair?: And Other Questions About Healthy Skin and Hair, Louise Spilsbury (Heinemann Library, 2003)

FURTHER RESEARCH

If you want to learn more about some of the topics covered in this book, why not investigate some of them further? Here are some ideas for your research:

• Eating disorders and what they do to the body.

• How the media influences our idea of beauty.

• What is happening inside the body during menstruation.

• Making homemade beauty treatments.

• Ayurveda, the Indian system of caring for the mind and body.

• The link between poor diet and disease.

• The importance of self-esteem.

GLOSSARY

abdominal muscles muscles of the stomach area

acne common skin disorder characterised by spots

anorexia eating disorder in which a person starves himself or herself

bacteria tiny creatures that can exist in the body and that cause infections and illness

bulimia eating disorder in which a person eliminates food from his or her body by vomiting and using laxatives

calorie measure of the amount of energy in food

cell tiniest building block of all living things

curfew specific time when a person, especially a young person, has to be back at home

diabetes incurable disease in which blood sugar levels are higher than normal. It can usually be controlled with diet and drugs.

digestive system system in the human body – including the oesophagus, stomach, intestines, and more – that works to digest food

emotional having to do with a person's feelings

empower give a feeling of strength

energy ability to do work

enhance improve the beauty of something

exfoliate scrub the skin with a gritty substance to remove dead skin cells

fibre part of fruits, vegetables, grains, nuts, seeds, and beans that the body cannot digest

gene hereditary unit that gives each individual his or her unique characteristics

high blood pressure disorder that can cause problems with the heart. It can usually be controlled with drugs.

hormone chemical produced by the body that regulates different body functions

hygiene personal cleanliness

menstruation shedding blood and cells from the lining of the uterus, the female organ that carries a baby. This shedding usually happens once a month.

mentor person who guides, advises, and supports a younger or less experienced person

nutrient substance in food that the body needs to function properly

obesity condition in which a person is more than 20 percent above normal body weight

peer class mate, work mate, or person in the same age group

peer pressure social pressure to behave or look a certain way

perspiration fluid lost from the body in the form of sweat

physical having to do with the body

pore tiny opening in the skin that hair grows out of

prejudice preformed belief that is not based on actual knowledge

premenstrual tension (PMT) common condition that occurs before or during menstruation and is characterized by pains, mood swings, and lack of energy

processed food food that contains dyes, artificial flavours, and other chemicals

puberty time of change in the body that makes it possible for reproduction to occur

purge get rid of undesirable substances. In the case of bulimia, the substance is food.

restore return something to its proper strength

self-conscious uncomfortable about yourself and your feelings

self-esteem person's confidence in his or her value as a person

SPF short for "sun protection factor". It is the measure of how much sun protection a suncream provides.

starter small portion of food, usually served before the main course

tone give strength and definition to

toxic shock syndrome serious condition that can be caused when a tampon is not changed regularly. Symptoms can include a high fever, headache, diarrhoea, and vomiting.

whole grain grain that has not had any part removed

Index